Instan

Instan

Cecilia Vicuña

Kelsey St. Press

Publication of this book was made possible by generous donations from the Friends of
the Collaboration Series. Special thanks to the LEF Foundation, Diane Middlebrook, Bar-
clay and Sharon Simpson, Sandra J. Springs, and Earlene Taylor.

Series produced by Rena Rosenwasser.

Library of Congress Cataloging-in-Publication Data
Vicuña, Cecilia.
Instan / Cecilia Vicuña. -- 1ˢᵗ ed.
p. cm.

ISBN: 0-932716-50-4 $15
ISBN: 0-932716-60-1 (50 signed limited editions
with an original drawing by the artist) $100
I. Title.
PQ8098.32.I35I57 2002
861'.64--dc21
2002010041

Kelsey St. Press   kelseyst.com

All orders to Small Press Distribution
510.524.1668
800.869.7553
orders@spdbooks.org

c o n t e n t s

instan

time

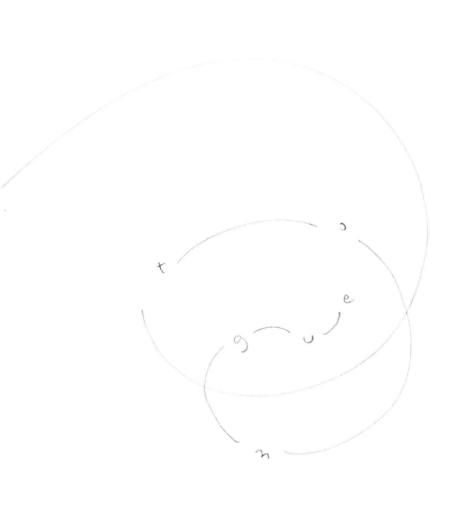

e

n

t

w

i

euhvine

the

n

e

t

h

e

b

d

c

o

v

t

b

dube

w

betwixt

l

e

i

x

t   t

thread

h

r

e

a

d

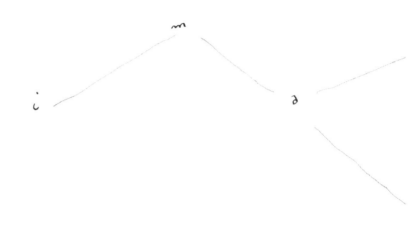

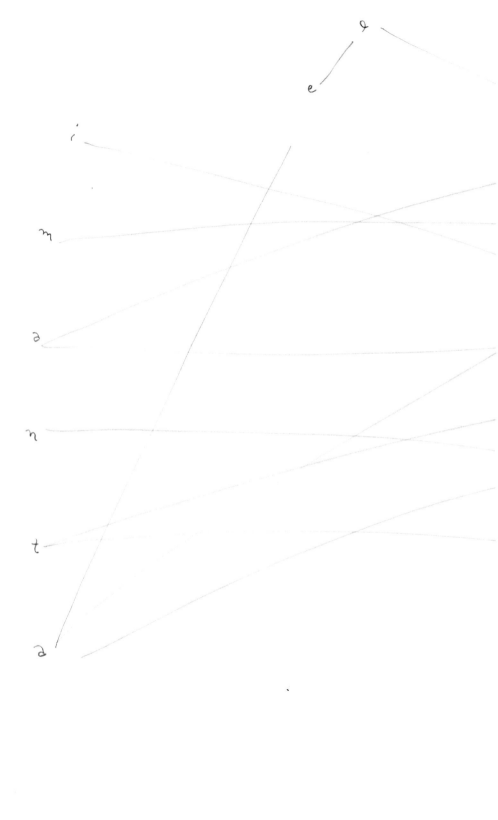

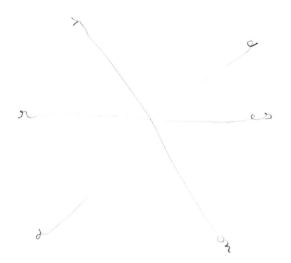

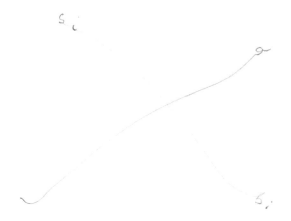

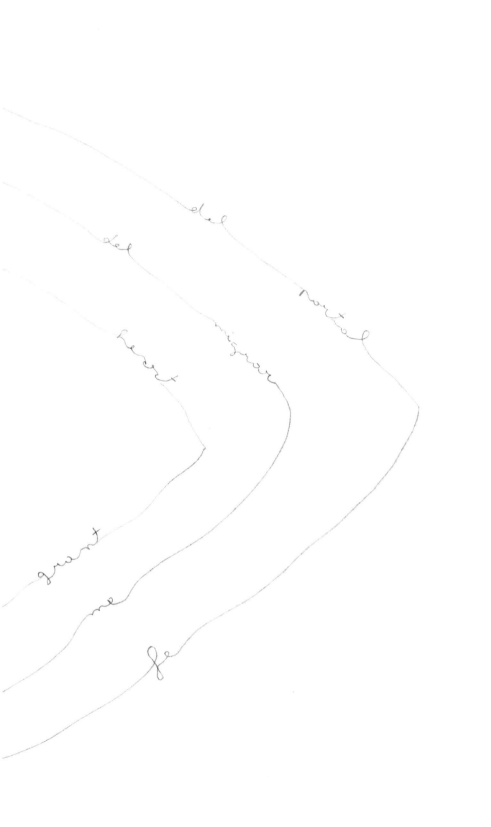

the   heart

care

lo tus llevo

del

llevo

...ffering of milk

cor venos fulgenter

light

of

veins

ole

un hi le de lig

m a

s e r

d e

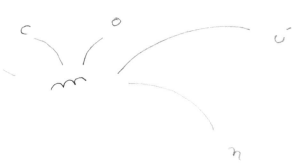

compass

com

rehend

rel

plement

pamion

miserate

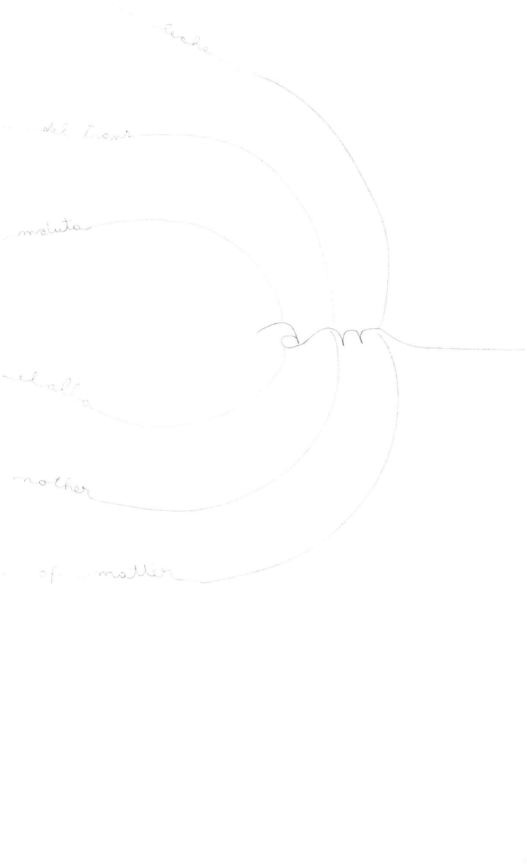

raíz de la mañana

el bien

mañana

manantial

el amar

early morning return

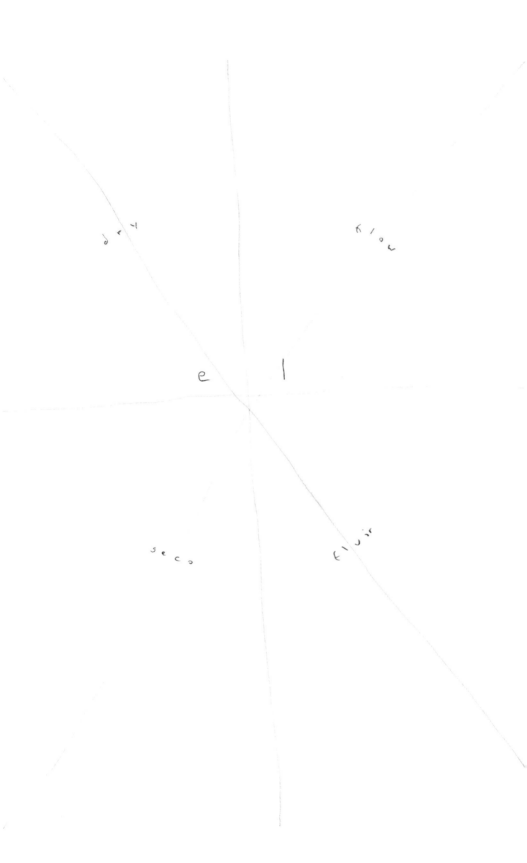

liquid

leaving

i   ir

ellipsis   eclipse

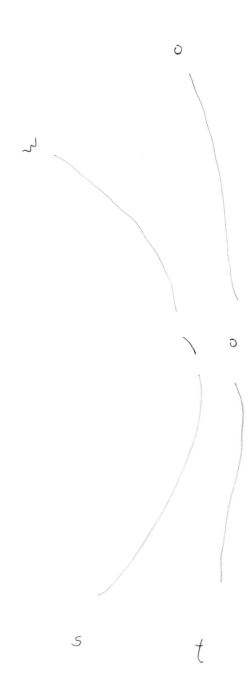

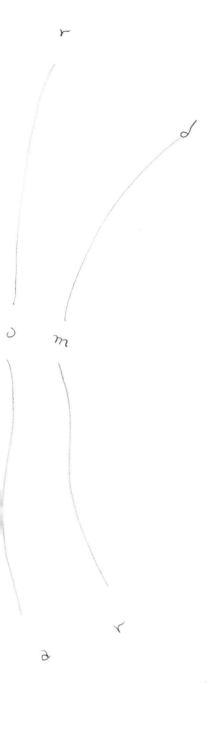

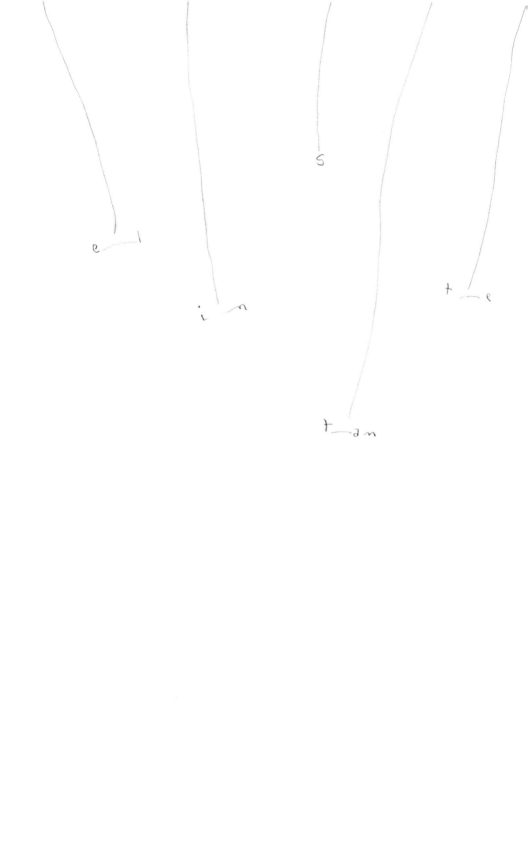

e

s

i n

t e

t an

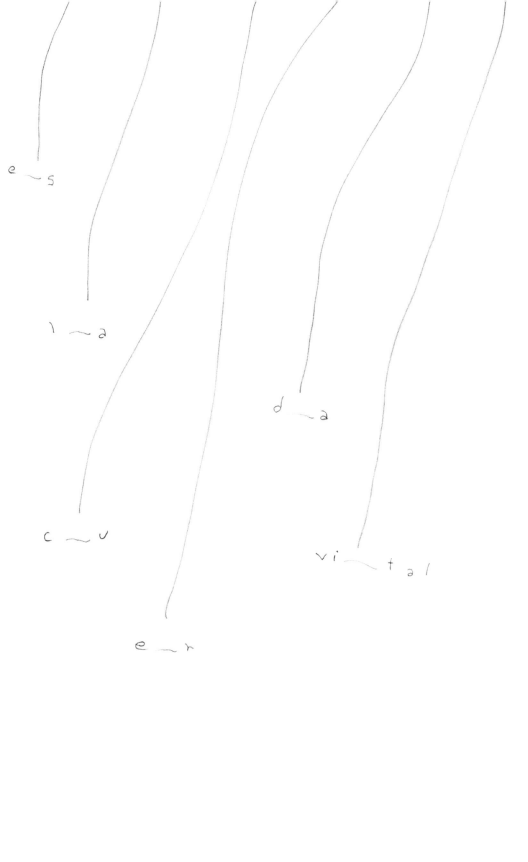

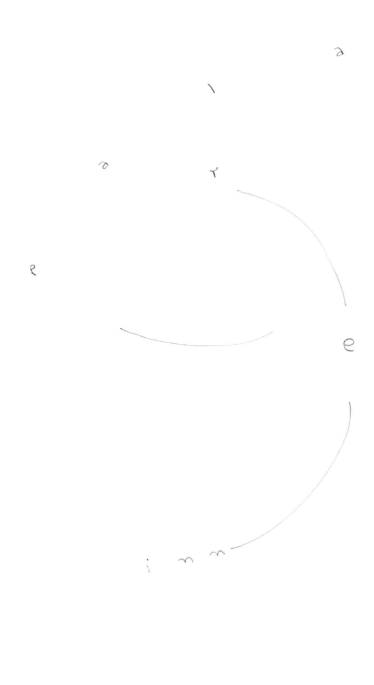

alba saliva
el instan

time bending
tongue

entwine
the betwixt

double
thread

madre
del habla

imán
del gen

palabra
estrella

mother
of time

el sign
                    o
no es
si no
insi
nua t
            ción

de la nube
en la nave
ga t
      ción

the nuance
of words

the mist
to go through

luz y del qué
the space
between words
imantando
el cruzar

crossing
magnet

respond
       e
sibila
¿cuál es
nuestra
ver dad?

¿por qué
est amos
a   quí?

the eye
is the I?

¿cuál
entre medio
es nues tro
lu   gar?

a pond
res ponds

libar
the way
you
re spond

corazón
del aquí

why are
we here?

luz del
portal

mei
del migrar

changed
heart

the in me
grant
            ing
me
life

un creer
en el core

changing
the heart
of the ear
                th

latus del
llevo llevo

mi sed
de un

futur
        o
re late

gramma
ticar

de un
recipro
cate

carry back
el re   late

la justicia
de la relación

de volver
el juguito
vital

¿adónde
la leche
de una
teta
común?

a com   mon
teat?

milk
del trans
late?

las venas
fulgentes
de un hilo
de luz?

a suckling
of musical
ink?

la her
mandad
de los rhythm
                    s
virtu
        e
            del
cog
    nate?

na   ser
del com
            ún?

ná ni ná
com
partir

ayni
el zumbar

a yarn
at full speed

deditos galaxias

el consejo
es el con
            s   tellation
of forms

a wetness
within

la mano
oyendo
un sudor

altas
y bajas
mar

el lápiz
me oye

la línea
oyendo
su manantial

amma

la leche
manando

amar
el formans

gramma
kellcani

draw
write
scratch

el silencio
y el ruidito
del lápiz

son mis
con se
jeros

las venas
del mundo
encantando
su salva t
          ción

.

escucha
el cimbrar

el instante
es la cuerda
vital

seco fluir
dry elixir

word
loom
star

life's
breath

el instan

estrella
interior

el
        e
            star.

fábulas del comienzo
y restos del origen

fables of the beginning
and remains of the origin

the great Expanse
in a tone Italic
of both worlds

Emily Dickinson

O pre-pensamento é o passado imediato do instante.

Clarice Lispector

tenderly, between the lines,
          bled, the lines.

Barbara Guest

Silence
      turns the page
            the poem begins.
                  alba del habla, the dawn of speech.

alquimia   del   nombre   alchemy   of   names

        el   instan

     palabra   fantasma

      sin   abrevar

  trans   mutation

    of   being.

"The soul co-authors the instant," Humberto Giannini says.

Time undone by the instant!

A *continuum* contradicted by name, time is "tem": to cut.

An instant is present,
      it "stands,"
        a filament of *sta,* a state of being, *stamen,*
a thread in a warp,
        a web in ecstasy.

"Being" is a compound of three forms: "to grow," "to set in
motion" and "yes, it may be so."
To be not an *estar,* but a way of being.

Hay que acompañar el hilo, "you have to accompany the thread,"
Don Pablo says, to pull and let go at once.

Awakening, the Buddha said: too loose it won't sing, too tight it will
snap.

Awareness awakens the thread?

In "awake" is *awak,* the Quechua "who weaves."
A way to awaken or to leave?

Time awakens inside words.

Awayo

mi

away!

Voy   a   tejer

mis   tres

lenguas   away.

Una lengua ve en la otra el interior del estar.

El poema se desvanece en el vórtice entre las dos.

Hedda Sterne said: "Art is not in the object, nor in the eye of the beholder, but in the meeting of both. This is the ambrosia that feeds the gods."

A word is a non-place for the encounter to take "place."

A continuous displacement, a field of "con," togetherness.

A word disappears, the connection remains.

Hear the image?   See the sound? The crossing performed?

Language: an enlightened form.

Oir la música de las cuerdas en tensión, la intención.

Let the fable begin:

El comienzo es el *com*, "with" in the beginning.

Turning with the stars.

A "uni verse" wants to *con* verse.

"Verse," to turn.

Galaxies and blood
Fingerprint whorls,
breath and sound.

Ibn Arabi dreamt he made love to the stars.

In this observatory words are stars,
the night sky I see,
and language, the spinner's view.

Is the spinner spun?

Cosmic fart, little gas?

Dialogar con lo que no es palabra al interior de las palabras crea
la unión.

Opening words I arrived at no word.

A moment of trance where transformation begins:
                                        silence to sound, and back.

An empty space within words where commingling occurs.

Abriendo palabras llegué a una inmensidad.

Our common being: Language, el ser de todos in speech.

Una línea de fuerza que se acrecienta con nuestro pasar. Algo
que vive en la lengua toda y emerge como el llamado de un ser.

To hear its hum, a tongue within tongues.

"Self" is "same," it says,
                    at once separate and not divisible from the whole.

"You and I are the same," it says,
                        our difference, a sound, tu per son.

> *Sounding the ten thousand things differently, so each becomes*
> *itself according to itself alone—who could make such music?*

Chuang Tzu, The Inner Chapters
translated by David Hinton

Per haps, *in di vi dual* says
                        un divided dual attention
                        un divided dual belonging

                            to itself and the whole at once.

Dis solve into union it says.
You will always be longing

my heart is what is not me
Antonin Artaud

Corazón del momento, el estar.

Corazón del tiempo, el instan.

imán   del   gen   nido del son

La lengua es la memoria de la especie, its po-ethical code,

a *com*mon ode.

A bond, as in *yuga, el juguito e'la unión,* yuxta posición.

Con jugate, not sub jugate.

"Justice" began as a ritual form, an exchange.

O así lo veía mi corazón embelesado en la *con* templación,
the temple of *con*
                          sciousness

          the fulcrum of change.

A possibility *con*tained in the name, a pre verbal form becoming
"com":
the handiwork of peace, the search for a *com*mon ground,

join with,   mutually comic,   c o l l e c t i v e l y.

En el *"con"* nacía el relato de una relación.

To carry back is to relate
                a flowing of milk: time
                                becomes language and love,

a grammar contained in *amma.*
                        el amor que congrega
                                    dice el guaraní

Una *gramma*tica fluía de la mama a la *gramma*:

                                la leche manando, la lengua y el
trans.

Hipnótico manar
                    the music of am
El am
        del am
                    or

no una idea abstracta
                        si no
                            una con
                                    ti nui
                                        dad.

Migrar y migrar y llegar al interior del estar.

We are only exiled from the inner e*star.*

                    Love in the genes, if it fails
                    We will produce no sane man again

                        George Oppen

/

Instan, el libro de la palabra estrella, is the journey inside the word *instan*.

It began as a night vision that landed on the page as a wave.

Intrigued, I went to the dictionary. *Instan* is the third person plural of the infinitive "instar," meaning "to urge, press, reply." It first appears in Spanish in 1490, and is associated with political demands. In English it means "to stud with stars."

For me it suggests a movement inward, towards the *sta,* the inner star "standing" in the verb "to be": estar.

In English, it presses the instant. Yet, the word did not wish to be just a door, it wanted to be a bridge between the two.

The poem was born as a cognate, *un cognado potens* in search of a middle ground, a language that would be readable or unreadable from both.

Acting as a riddle, each word gave birth to the next, opening up to reveal ancient or future meanings.

Instan was *hatunsimi,* a pregnant word in Quechua: "La palabra preñada que salen muchas de ella." (Diego González Holguin, *Vocabulario de la Lengua General de Todo el Peru, llamada Lengua Quichua o del Inca,* Cuzco, 1608.)

The question feeds the enigma: an echo sent to the Milky Way, *Wiraqochan,* moves simultaneously towards the future and the past. It regenerates the vital force and returns as milk and blood, semen and fat.

.

d i x i o
            n a r y   a   d i c t i o n

alba: dawn, white, first light, ritual dress, a palindrome of habla, speech. Divining through echoes, the Incas composed crucial words as palindromes: *wiñay qallallallaq pacha,* the fertility of all generations.

imán: magnet; from the Latin diamond, *adimas.*

imán del gen: image(n). The image as the magnet of genes.

imantar: magnetize, imantando, magnetizing.

palabra: word; from the Latin *parabola,* comparison.

estrella: star; Latin *stella.*

insinuación: insinuation.

navegación: navigation.

luz: light, from the Latin *lux.*

qué: what; Latin *quid.*

sibila: sibyl; Greek *Sibulla,* woman regarded as an oracle.

verdad: truth; in Latin *veritas, verax.*

aquí: here.

estamos: we are, from estar, to be.

entremedio: inter middle, in between.

lugar: place, Latin *locus*.

libar: libation, to pour, to make an offering to the gods, the oldest meaning of the verb "to respond."

corazón: heart; Latin *cor*.

mei del migrar: *mei*, the root of change, *gra*, "heart," "migrant": "changed heart."

latus: to carry, as in *relatus*: relate, translate.

llevo llevo: carry carry. Canoe carriers in the Amazon announce their trade shouting "llevo llevo" (canoes are the taxis on the river).

sed: thirst.

grammaticar: a word made up from the Greek *gramma*, to scratch, draw and write, and the Spanish ending of a verb.

leche: milk, latte.

venas: veins.

fulgentes: "full of people" (gente is people), but no, it really means *relampaguear*, to flash with lightning.

hermandad: the un-gendered noun for sister/brotherhood, from the Latin *germen*.

ná ni ná: no more. A Chilean/Andalusian style expression echoed by the Quechua *na*, I don't remember anymore, *na*, I suddenly remember again.

compartir: to share.

ayni: Quechua, to reciprocate.

zumbar: onomatopeia for the sound of the spinning thread.

consejo: counsel, advice, council.

oyendo un sudor: hearing a sweat. We know in sweat before we know in "words." (Instant knowledge).

altas y bajas mar: high and low tide.

el lápiz me oye: the pencil hears me.

la línea oyendo su manantial: the line hears its spring.

amma: palindrome of *ma*, the Proto Indo-European root for "good," "morning," and "mother." Also, "Matuta" the goddess of dawn and the Latin *amare* to love.

formans: "a bunch of frequencies in the human voice" says Carlos Guedes.

kellcani: Quechua verb, writing and drawing.

ruidito: little noise.

cimbrar: to sway.

cuerda: cord or chord.

I drew-wrote this book
between 1995 and
2002, while travelling
between New York
and Buenos Aires,
Santiago, and the
Southern Andes, and
during a brief stay at
the Fundación Val-
paraiso in Murxis Akra
(Mojácar) in the
Mediterranean.

This book is for
my mother,
sweet milk,
Norma Ramírez, Estrel-
la del sur, Chakana. For
my
father Jorge Vicuña,
the eyes that see,
Alpha Beta Centauri,
Llamacñawin.
Both aspects of
la Pachamama.
For César Paternosto,
mi bien estar.
For Rosa Alcalá,
translator of more
than milk.
And the poets at
Kelsey St. Press,
who asked for it.

To all of them
my gratitude.

INSTAN is a
limited edition
of one thousand five
hundred copies; fifty
are numbered and
signed by the artist
and include an
original drawing
on Hahnemühle
Heine Smooth paper.
It was produced by
West Coast Print
Center on Coronado
White Vellum Text.
The text is set in
Gill Sans.
Book design by
Robert Rosenwasser.

Kelsey St. Press
2002